SandCastle

Word Families Set 4

-uff as in cuff

Nancy Tuminelly

Consulting Editor Monica Marx, M.A./Reading Specialist

ABDO Publishing Company

Published by SandCastle™, an imprint of ABDO Publishing Company, 4940 Viking Drive, Edina, Minnesota 55435.

Printed in the United States.

Credits
Edited by: Pam Price
Curriculum Coordinator: Nancy Tuminelly
Cover and Interior Design and Production: Mighty Media
Photo Credits: Brand X Pictures, Corbis Images, Hemera, PhotoDisc, Stockbyte

Library of Congress Cataloging-in-Publication Data

Tuminelly, Nancy, 1952-
       -Uff as in cuff / Nancy Tuminelly.
         p. cm. -- (Word families. Set IV)
       Summary: Introduces, in brief text and illustrations, the use of the letter combination "uff" in such words as "cuff," "fluff," "huff," and "stuff."
       ISBN 1-59197-246-9
       1. Readers (Primary) [1. Vocabulary. 2. Reading.] I. Title.

PE1119 .T835 2003
428.1--dc21   2002038639

SandCastle™ books are created by a professional team of educators, reading specialists, and content developers around five essential components that include phonemic awareness, phonics, vocabulary, text comprehension, and fluency. All books are written, reviewed, and leveled for guided reading, early intervention reading, and Accelerated Reader® programs and designed for use in shared, guided, and independent reading and writing activities to support a balanced approach to literacy instruction.

Let Us Know

After reading the book, SandCastle would like you to tell us your stories about reading. What is your favorite page? Was there something hard that you needed help with? Share the ups and downs of learning to read. We want to hear from you! To get posted on the ABDO Publishing Company Web site, send us e-mail at:

sandcastle@abdopub.com

SandCastle Level: Transitional

-uff Words

bluff

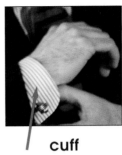

cuff

fluff

huff

puff

stuff

3

Mom and Dad stood
on the bluff.

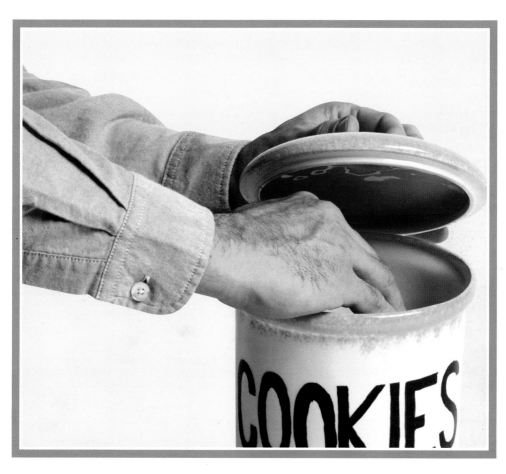

Mr. Adams has a
button on his cuff.

The bear's hat has a
ball of fluff.

Joy walked away
from her dad in a huff.

A cream puff is a
yummy treat.

Allie has a lot of stuff in her room.

Too Much Stuff

In a house
high on a bluff

lived a family whose
name was Tuff.

Mr. Tuff got very gruff.

He said his family has
too much stuff.

Jen Tuff was in a huff.

Her dad said,
"Get rid of some stuff!"

Jen had a cat named Fluff,

who just sat
on top of her stuff.

Mr. Tuff said
to Ben, "It's time
that we got rid
of some stuff."

But Ben just sat

and dreamed
of a cream puff.

Mr. Tuff had enough.

He just started
to throw away stuff.

Then he began
to huff and puff.

But all he did
was scare poor Fluff!

The -uff Word Family

bluff	Mr. Tuff
buff	puff
cuff	scruff
fluff	scuff
gruff	snuff
huff	stuff

Glossary

Some of the words in this list may have more than one meaning. The meaning listed here reflects the way the word is used in the book.

bluff   a cliff or other steep piece of land

cuff   a fold at the end of a shirt sleeve

gruff   a rough or harsh manner of speech or action

huff   a short period of being upset or annoyed; to breathe out strongly

puff   something light and fluffy; a short burst of air or smoke

About SandCastle™

A professional team of educators, reading specialists, and content developers created the SandCastle™ series to support young readers as they develop reading skills and strategies and increase their general knowledge. The SandCastle™ series has four levels that correspond to early literacy development in young children. The levels are provided to help teachers and parents select the appropriate books for young readers.

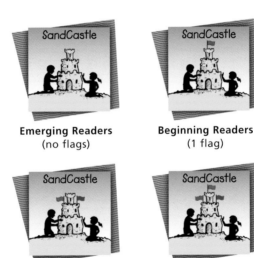

Emerging Readers
(no flags)

Beginning Readers
(1 flag)

Transitional Readers
(2 flags)

Fluent Readers
(3 flags)

These levels are meant only as a guide. All levels are subject to change.

To see a complete list of SandCastle™ books and other nonfiction titles from ABDO Publishing Company, visit www.abdopub.com or contact us at:

4940 Viking Drive, Edina, Minnesota 55435 • 1-800-800-1312 • fax: 1-952-831-1632